PORTRAIT

PORTRAIT

Poems by

Gillian Lynn Katz

Illustrations by Patricia Frankel
Cover design by Shay Culligan

ISBN: 978-1-950462-70-4

Kelsay Books Inc.

kelsaybooks.com

502 S 1040 E, A119
American Fork,Utah 84003

Also by Gillian Lynn Katz

Witness to the Birth and Death of my Country
Collection of poetry, fiction and essays on South Africa

Kaleidoscope
Poetry chapbook

For Ken, Melissa and Ashley
I hold you in my heart, forever.

Acknowledgments

Midnight Second Place Winner in the Greenburgh Poetry Contest published *in Let the Poets Speak* 2012; and in Magnum Opus Worldwide Anthology, India 2019
My Johannesburg Best Emerging Poets of New York 2017, Anthology, Z Publishing
Mugabe and the White African Austin International Poetry Festival Anthology 2017

Finishing Line Press published her chapbook *Kaleidoscope* in 2012 These poems were included in that book: (additional magazine publications are indicated).

The Pale Green Sertificaat from the Union of South Africa
Egoli The Westchester Review 2013
Scarsdale ephiphmag.com Issue 15 August 2012
Retrospective SUB MAG Issue 64, Purchase College, NY
Chicken Run Inkwell 1997, Manhattanville College; The Tom Howard Anthology *Across the Long Bridge* in 2006
Tin Cup, Tin Plate The Westchester Review 2013
Pendulum's Justice Autumn 2005 issue of Fling Quarterly, Sarah Lawrence College
Adjudication Poetry Master Ink Anthology 2012 edited by Dan Masterson
Rita Rains on the Big Easy SUB MAG Issue 63, Purchase College, NY
Ode to the Fish Who Nibbled Bin Laden's Brain Italics Mine, Issue 3.1, Purchase College, NY
Mystical Ephiphanies Italics Mine, Issue 14, Purchase College, NY
Chiaroscuro (appeared in different form in Kaleidoscope)
Philanderer Autumn 2005 Issue of Fling Quarterly, Sarah Lawrence College
No Crosses, Please September 2005 issue No 65 of Ambassador Watch, New Zealand

Additional Publications

Homesickness Italics Mine, Issue 14, Purchase College, NY
The Search For Noah's Ark SUB MAG Issue 63, Purchase College, NY
Portrait *Let the Poets Speak* Greenburgh Poetry Contest 2013
Hands *Let the Poets Speak* Greenburgh Poetry Contest 1999

—

Contents

POT POURRI

MOTHERHOOD

ANGST

SOUTH AFRICA

The Pale Green Sertificaat from the Union of South Africa

My birth certificate states
I am female.

My identified Christian name
Gillian Lynn

and Bagg, my family's surname
also on the certificate.

The race of my parents:
European. Their names

are not recorded. Whoever
gave me life, is not important.

This certificate merely states
that I am free to roam

by the color of my skin
not like the Bantu, Indians,

Asians and half-breeds
who aren't allowed

to call our South Africa
Home.

eGoli

Zulu name for City of Gold, Johannesburg

The leaping arc of linked impala
a sculpture curved
over a rainbow fountain
has been stolen
piece by piece.

Hacksawed, sold as scrap metal
in the New South Africa.

Oppenheimer Park in Johannesburg
built between President and Prichard Streets
before the bloodless revolution

stands empty.

Scarsdale

A golden girl, I picked lavender
Jacaranda blossoms
that tumbled
onto Johannesburg grasses.

As a pink-collared working woman
I watched white Dogwood flowers
cover the Tarrytown trees in masses.

Now, as flame-colored azaleas burst forth
every Scarsdale spring,
I still feel the
thunderclap:
the cloudburst that blew
a flower petal
across two continents.

Retrospective

The trees I sit under are rain-drenched
leafy. I am two continents,
forty-five years away.
On my computer, an image—
A resplendent European Roller—
not one color missing on that bird;
Perched on a dried out tree twig
in the Kruger National Park
on the Facebook page
of a classmate
I'd long since forgotten.

Yesterday—Today and Tomorrow

"Yesterday, Today and Tomorrow"—
The name of the flower, purple and blue
in Johannesburg gardens of my youth.

Now that I'm grown those flowers are gone.
I'll never see that shade of blue
Today, another day, or tomorrow.

So far away, the climate has changed
and now the flowers are a different hue
from the colorful gardens of my youth.

I never knew I'd travel so far
leave my homeland forever, no clue
yesterday, today or tomorrow.

My grandparents showed me those flowers
that sparkled in the morning dew
in Johannesburg gardens of my youth.

Now the gardens have changed
There'r different things I do
In Scarsdale gardens
I have a new truth.

Chicken Run

When I was a child
my mother hid a nanny
in her walk-in cupboard
behind expensive dresses
that smelled
of sweet perfume,
so the South African police
wouldn't find her
because she didn't have
a passbook.

My father taught me
to ask politely
for a glass of water
from the brown rounded nannies
in white overalls and headrags
who swept our *stoep*
and cooked our food.

Black men drove in green lorries
and rode on rickety bicycles
through the streets
of Johannesburg.
They wore khaki uniforms
when they watered our
gardens.

A black woman sniffed out of
a large tin of snuff
as she dug the weeds
with a screwdriver.

Apartheid: the policy
of the white heat
of the Kimberley Diamond
ruling over the black coal
of Sasol
as crude as the oil
pumped
from your smoky pollution.
I am the product of an oligarchy
and you have robbed me of
my senses.

Apartheid: you have clipped my wings
so I cannot fly across the mine dumps,
the immense flat-topped white sand dunes
on the edge of the Golden City,
where black men plummet
down mine shafts thousands of feet deep;
where the air is as close as an oven
and vision as black as night,
as black as the men
who dig gold out of rocks
for their Johannesburg masters.

Apartheid: you have torn me from my roots,
the sunbaked grassland where the baobab tree
with is gnarled arms
like large octopus tentacles
reaches
into the burnt orange sky,
its trunk as thick as an elephant.
Fever trees poise like a flat
green umbrella against the red and gold
sunset.

You have stabbed me through my heart
with your African spear
as sharp as the shimmering
translucent crystal formations
that rise and fall
in the Cango caves.

You have stopped my ears so I cannot
hear the roar of the lion at dawn,
after his mate has killed a zebra
by the waterhole at Kruger Park,
where hyena wait to feed
and vultures circle.

The tidal wave
of the first Chicken Run
swept us away
like the white grains
of sand on Durban beach.

Apartheid: we were seeds
you held in your fist,
and shook with the thunder
of a Transvaal lightning storm,
flinging us out in the wind
to the four corners
of the Earth.

The first group
of white chickens ran
after the 1960 Sharpeville massacre
where hundreds of blacks
peacefully protesting
the pass laws
were shot in the back
as they fled the police.

We were the first wave of whites
to escape.
We left by train on May 2, 1966
a train that took us not to
Buchenwald or Dachau—
but to Cape Town, where blue mountains
rise majestically out of the green sea
that hugs the foot of Africa,
and Table Mountain sits flat-topped,
covered by a white table cloth
on a cloudy day.

We sailed on a ship where the green
Indian Ocean
joins the blue Atlantic
and on to New York
where the Statue of Liberty
lifts her freedom torch
to the sky.
More whites left on the second
Chicken Run in 1976
when police murdered black
school children who were protesting
the use of Afrikaans in their education,
the language of the oppressor
who pushed their leaders
out of tenth floor
prison windows—
saying they had
committed suicide.

Apartheid:
you have beaten the drums
of the Zulu warrior
with black on black violence
in the temperate province of Natal

where the ANC and Inkatha Parties
murder each other's children.
Then again, in the 1980's—
thousands of white families
scattered
in another Chicken Run.

In the New South Africa whites live
behind high fences with burglar alarms,
their manicured lawns
and mansions concealed.
It is common to ask a neighbor or a
friend
which brand of barbed wire will keep
out the mass
of starving blacks who would kill
for a piece of bread.
Which gun is the best for your wife
or daughter to wear in her
brassiere?

Apartheid: you have exploded
like the whirling mass of water of
the Augrabies Falls and gouged out
a deep hole in the heart of my
country—
washed the treasure of diamonds:
your people—
down the Orange River.

You have scattered your citizens
like the blossoms that fall
off the Jacaranda tree—
not to form purple carpets
outside plush homes in Johannesburg
or in the streets of Pretoria—
but scattered in the wind
to the ends of the Earth.

Tin Cup, Tin Plate

A white girl with white hands
places a tin cup of milk tea
and four sugars
on the back door step
of her family's house.
And a tin plate with sliced bread
(each piece thick as a brick)
smothered in raspberry jam.

The garden boy, Phineas,
eats behind the house
sitting on the ground.
White sheets flap
above him
on the washline.

The white girl stays locked in
behind barred windows.
Alarm wires thinly strung
across transparent panes.

Broken glass
cemented into high stone walls
surround, protect,
her childhood home.

And Phineas sits
in the backyard.
The white sheets flap
above him
on the washline.

Pendulum's Justice

I once lived in a mansion
in sunny South Africa
with rolling green lawns
and blue Hydrangea flowers
whose large mauve heads
danced
in the warm summer breeze.

I was waited on by servants.

Thirty years later, I live
in a two-bedroom
apartment
in Tarrytown, New York.

I am engulfed by a blizzard.
Washing loads of laundry
baby slides down my leg
as her sister runs round me
in circles.

My address in Johannesburg
was Number Six
Fifteenth Avenue
Lower Houghton.
Nelson Mandela's
Presidential Palace
is on Thirteenth Avenue
Lower Houghton.

Just think—
if we hadn't emigrated
the President and I
could have been
neighbors.

But late at night
I cannot rest
with infant kicking
my stomach
and her tiny fist
pounding
my naked breast.

I steal time to write
like the servants
stole bread
in my mansion.

Black Magic

I was eight years old when The Royal Ballet of London
came to Johannesburg.

Three of the ballerinas visited us: Janet, Ian and Sheila.
Janet and Ian were married. We have home movies of them
pirouetting into our pool.

A special night was reserved for the natives. My mother drove
our three servants: Betty and Sonny and Kobus
to His Majesty's Theatre in the center of Johannesburg.

Mommy gave Betty and Sonny two of her own
colorful dresses, coats, new leather shoes
and matching handbags.
My father gave Kobus one of his old suits
with a new tie. Kobus wore the black lace-up shoes
he'd polished for my father every morning
for the past five years.

Mommy handed them money to each buy their own
Black Magic chocolate box to eat during the performance.
She waited until the performance was over
and drove them back home to our house.
They lived in tiny rooms in our backyard.

    The next day they all walked out on her.
    They didn't even quit.
    They just disappeared back
    into the black hole of the townships
    without having their passbooks signed.
    They'd been part of our family forever.

Tokoloshi

a hairy imp that hexes you in the dark of night

I thought we were kindred spirits
I, too, am a white child of Africa.
You damaged my work with website hits
now that we're both living in America.

I, too, am a white child of Africa.
You and I are not the same
now that we're both living in America.
Apartheid blood still runs in your veins.

You and I are not the same
when I reach out across the sea.
Apartheid blood still runs in your veins
because you try to silence me.

When I reach out across the sea
To tell compatriots what this ex-pat feels—
Because you try to silence me
You're a bastard, a thief and a heel.

To tell compatriots what this ex-pat feels
It took me decades to learn the craft of words
You're a bastard, a thief and a heel.
You thought that I would be deterred.

It took me decades to learn the craft of words
And now I'm going to sue you in court.
You thought that I would be deterred
I never dreamed this would be a battle I fought.

And now I'm going to sue you in court
So maybe now you'll finally learn
I never dreamed this would be a battle I fought
Prestige and dignity have to be earned.

So maybe now you'll finally learn
You can't hide behind internet crime
Prestige and dignity have to be earned
And the words I have written: they are all mine.

I trusted you, I thought we were friends
You damaged my work with website hits.
Now our relationship has to end.
I thought we were kindred spirits.

Adjudication

For Thyrza Lombard

In the New South Africa
the Xhosa Sangoma genuflected,
threw bones on the dusty green
carpet by the handwoven
Lesotho rug,
in the bedroom of the cottage,
the white woman's
deathplace.

Mashinini the son of her garden worker
strangled her lifeblood
with a shoelace.

She penned checks for his uniforms
and education,
bailed his father out jail
in the Old South Africa.

In the New South Africa
the Xhosa Sangoma chanted
and prayed by the handwoven
Lesotho rug
put a curse on Mashinini
to spend the rest of his life
in prison. The white woman's
children
paid the Sangoma
four thousand rands.

Mashinini got twenty years
in the New South Africa
for murdering his mentor
on the Lesotho woolen rug
woven with ancient
tribal hands.

My Johannesburg

I weep for you Johannesburg,
you are the city of my birth.
You had the trendiest suburb
but now you are devoid of mirth.
Violence and murders and racial hatred
leave your buildings dilapidated.

When Nelson Mandela was released from prison,
we thought it would heal the racial schism . . .
Instead there's an increase in poverty and AIDS
carjackings and murders replace police raids.
My heart used to break from leaving Africa,
Now I'm gladder than ever to be in America.

Our New South Africa was supposed to work
Please, don't leave my homeland in squalor and dirt.

A Drumbeat Cure for AIDS

In a searing agony
plant the seed of death
between the thighs
of a South African
baby girl.

This will cure your
    AIDS
Raping a virgin
    will cure your
    AIDS.

Not American AZT
    Not the drugs
        you refuse.

You say
    its dispensed
        to control
            the third world
                people.

Your superstition
    and *muti*
        your witchcraft
            your rape...

This will cure you
    of AIDS.

And the baby girl?

Mugabe and the White African

for Michael Campbell
in memoriam

A petrol fire burnt the fertile fields
of Zimbabwe. Mugabe's murderers
beat the soles of his feet
as he lost his livelihood.
The Court commanded
Michael Campbell keep
his farm on Mount Carmel.
Why was his family slaughtered?
Must madmen massacre white Africans?

Systematically they set fires
round his stone-and-thatch farmhouse
and burned his Biri River Safari Lodge
in a dusty hot heat haze
they slaughtered
giraffe, impala, gamebirds
white tailed wildebeest
and warthogs.

They cursed, they cut,
they cracked his skull
a color blind man
in love with his country.
They cut down his crops
the lush groves of mangoes
festered in a rutted dirt track
rotted to purplish pulp
in the pack sheds.

And Rhodesia the breadbasket of Africa
lies barren as millions mourn, malnourished.

Homesickness

I want to jump through my computer screen, where I see my cousins on Facebook. I haven't seen them in the flesh since 1984. When I crash through the curtains of light that separate us, the particles of the sun repose me onto the promenade of Plettenberg Bay. I am with them in the now: Jimmy, Sonja, Maisie, Todd, as we bicycle down the coastline of Cape Town. Gone are the snowbanks of New York. The streets covered in black ice where I slip and slide on the driveway, plows that sift the sodden soggy saturated snow into mountains of mush on the sidewalks.

Now, the only mountain I see is Table Mountain, its flat-topped peak shrouded by a lacy cloth of clouds covering its circumference. I want to hail the halcyon days of deliverance where cousin can be with cousin. We are no longer separated by oceans of water and millennia of minutes, but we dive with the dolphins and swim with the sharks where the azure blue waves crash into the shore.

We dance through the dryness of the Karoo and run with the rhinos. We watch the water buffalo and we wait for the lions at Kruger Park. We hail the hydrangeas as they bloom by the boughs of the bougainvillea. We smell the sweet lilac of the winding wisteria and wile under the weeping willows. We pick mangoes off the trees that grow in our gardens. The cherry blossoms that give way to gorgeous red and yellow fruits and mulberry trees, dozens of them that grow down the hill towards the grapevine where Jack, the Bantu servant who had been with my grandparents for decades grew *dagga,* a stronger strain than American marijuana. All these days and nights where I can commune with my compatriots. I don't have to wait for the jumbo jet that will carry me back to my country. I will dream again of golden days I left in migratory madness.

Gugulethu

Simphiwe drove us in a fire engine red van
when we toured the bustling township
in the Western Cape
of South Africa.
Gugulethu, contraction of *igugu lethu,*
in Xhosa, means: our pride.

The tribe
trademarked by *ukwaluka,* male
circumcision at eighteen.
Their language has three different
click sounds which Luyolo demonstrated
in the sentence: *I learned to shave the old man's head.*
My American born daughter cheered.

I told Simphiwe he looked like Sydney Poitier.
He'd never heard of the actor, and said:
I will have to kill him.
His handsome face shone with a smile so we knew
this was a joke, the same kind of joke our beloved nanny Daisy,
who'd been with the family for twenty years
told my mother: Comes the Revolution, I will go next door and kill
the madam there. And the girl from next door will come and kill you.
But the revolution never came.
Nelson Mandela made peace
between the ninety-five percent blacks
and five percent whites.

Botlierskop

I walked with two female lions
at the Reserve in Mossel
Bay. Each of us carried
a clubbed stick,
were told never to turn
our backs towards the beasts.

When the lions stopped to rest,
the guide photographed
us, one by one,
with our own I-Phones.

The Xhosa tribesman
held my hand all the way
up the rocks
so I could perch behind
the resting giants.

The guide tapped
the ground with a long stick
to indicate
the place
where I should stand
far back,

so his compatriot
could land
the perfect portrait.

Robben Island

Nelson, I walked where you walked,
for three hours,
inside gray cement walls,
where you chopped snow white quarry stones
in the heat, Mandela,
on the windy prison island
surrounded by the sea.

Swaths of black kelp meandered
in the ocean floating free
like you wouldn't be, Nelson.

I stood outside your cell, Mandela,
Four-square-meter circumference
where you spent eighteen
of your twenty seven-year sentence.

You slept on a straw pallet on the stone floor:
brown blanket, small green table,
red bucket with a lid.
Your walls and door were steel see-through bars.

More prince
than prisoner, dressed neatly
in prison clothes, leaning on a spade.
You sealed your scrolls
buried them in tin cans
in a small garden with only an aloe bush
surrounded by gray cement walls.

Inside Mandela's Former Penitentiary

A single oleander inside grey stone prison walls:

A flash of pink blooms in clusters
deep green leathery lance-shaped leaves
arranged along the stems in whorls.

I wonder, did you witness the ache
of this poisonous plant
when you were ordered not to sing
as you cut the snow white
rocks in the lime quarry?

The Footprint of God

In an isolated area in Mpaluzi,
close to the Swaziland border,
a two hundred million-year-old
footprint,

four feet high in rough granite,
imprinted against the side of the rock,
each toe perfectly proportioned,
slope of the foot, down to the heel.

At the top of the toes, an overhang
of rough granite, when the giant lifted
his foot off the floor
in the Eastern Transvaal
of South Africa.

IN THE NEWS

Rohingya

Tens of thousands
displaced by monsoons
wade waist high through sludgy waters:
Migration from Myanmar,
escaping terror.

Groups of brown skinned men
gathered like grapes,
grasp bottles of water.
Women sit on stones,
in a semblance of saris.

A cluster of children claw
tin and plastic bowls
like hats doffed in supplication
waiting for their daily dose
of sustenance.

One of every hundred and fifteen people
on the planet is a refugee.
And one day, Sir, it could be you,
or me.

Rita Rains on the Big Easy

On a downtown New Orleans avenue
the gray high-rises echo.
A silver van stands parked
near the sidewalk.

On the street a lone man stands
       half-naked,
in a red bathing suit
with white flowers.

He raises his arms skywards,
outstretched, palms upwards;
his face towards the grey-white sky.

The Littlest Wave

Seismic tsunami waves shook
the Indian Ocean, the force
of an atom bomb.

A thirty foot wave exploded
crashed into one hundred and fifty
thousand people, killing them;
and thousands more missing.

A baby boy found floating on a mattress
a note pinned to his blanket.
The nurses hid him from human
traffickers who sell children for sex.
They treasured and mothered him
called him "Little Wave."

"The last unclaimed orphan"
at a hospital in Phuket.

After The Storm

a wet piano that still plays   and floats

a family Bible passed through five generations   washed out

his son's birth announcement   printing smeared but not lost

                    floor boards piled on the lawn

          soggy, saturated   baby carriages

          drenched photograph albums

          a wasted wedding dress
mounds of molding trash   stinking

                                        submerged
tens of thousands of Texans
wading in water up to their waists
                                in gray
                          storm waters

impaired foundations
                    appliances, television sets and home décor

          in neighborhoods both affluent and poor.

rapids
                              from three feet of water

beginning to desert a city
                    sputtering back to life

                    red ants and crocodiles
                                in   Harvey's Houston

Hurricane Irma

I'm watching Chris Cuomo and Anderson
Cooper on CNN pounded with rainwater,
winds blowing, trees bowing
backwards and forwards and backwards again.
The commentators keep commenting.
My niece is somewhere in a high rise. Power is out.
We can't contact her. Elderly Dan and Miriam are hunkered down,
on the second floor of a building. The last tenants
who didn't leave.
Chris Cuomo and Anderson Cooper
talk loudly to the camera.
How does the cameraman
keep dry? How much do these guys get paid
to be pummeled and shaken in the eye of a hurricane?
Chris Cuomo has lost his hat,
his face is streaming with water. His microphone
is still working. Is it attached to a sound system that hasn't
drowned? Hours go by, hours, and still we haven't' heard
from Betsy and Miriam and Dan, and all these people
who sent me pictures of garbage cans racing down
the highway in the wind.

The Shakespeare Riot

at the Astor Opera House in New York City,
May 7, 1849
broke out
because the first American theatrical star Edwin Forrest
and the greatest British actor of his generation
William Charles Macready
both played the Scottish King.

The audience cheered when the American actor spoke Macbeth's line:
What rhubarb, senna or what purgative drug will scour these English
hence?

The British actor's performance of Macbeth
was brought to a halt by American fans
who threw rotten eggs, potatoes, apples, lemons, shoes, bottles of piss
shouting: *Down with the codfish aristocracy.*

Macready was to flee back home
when a petition signed by Herman Melville and Washington Irving
persuaded him to stay:
the good sense of the community
would respect his right to perform.

The state's Seventh Regiment assembled in Washington Square Park
mounted troops, artillery and hussars, a total of three hundred and fifty
men
and hundreds more inside and outside the theatre
couldn't protect the homes of the city's wealthy and elite.

Handbills and posters littered:
Shall Americans or English Rule This City?

The next day the *New York Tribune* reported
one window after another cracked.
Bricks and paving stones rattled
the civilized community.
The Opera House resembled a fortress besieged.

Two centuries later, the riots continue
against immigrants taking American jobs.

Internet Exposure

Every time I open my AOL
to view my emails,
Jeffrey Epstein's forlorn face
peers at me from my computer.

I don't want to see
he was found with neck injuries
in his prison cell
from a possible
suicide attempt.

He, and all the child traffickers,
sex offenders, terrorists, baby killers, murderers,
horrors from around the globe

assault me, in my quiet office
alone in the suburbs
in the beauty and solitude
of my *Leave it to Beaver*
life.

Ode to the Fish Who Nibbled Bin Laden's Brain

A gray and white striped Scizzortail
undulated through his bullet holed head;
paused its sinuous swirl,
and kissed the mouth for a second.
A king angelfish entered
through the eye socket
from the other direction.
The angelfish bumped
into the brain's pulpy flesh,
nibbled the hanging tendrils
and swam through the blasted out
ear canal, back
into the Arabian Sea's dark thunder.

Pigcasso

Step Aside Francis Bacon:
a rescued pig paints on a canvas
at the Farm Sanctuary in Franschhoek
outside Cape Town in South Africa.

The limited-edition *Flying Pig by Ms. Pigcasso*
features green, blue and pink brush strokes
and sells for one hundred and twenty dollars:
Proceeds go to animal rescue.

Brandishing a paintbrush with her snout,
Pigcasso tosses her head with enthusiasm
to create bright, bold brushstrokes
across a canvas,
propped up in her sty.

The sow was rescued from an abattoir
as a piglet and brought to an animal
sanctuary. Her new owners noticed
her love of color and paintbrushes.
Pigs are smart animals:
the owner needed to keep her
entertained.

They threw in soccer and rugby balls
but the pig ate or destroyed them, except
for the paintbrushes
which she used as an abstract
expressionist, her style
slightly changing,
depending on her mood,
like any great artist.

The Search for Noah's Ark

A team of Texas archeologists
looked for clues historians missed,
to find the remains of Noah's ark and bring
scripture out of the dark.

Was the ark made out of gopher,
a wood so strange,
buried in the Elburz range?
Or was it hidden
under a snow-capped peak
hundreds of feet
upon Mount Ararat?

Up, thirteen thousand feet archeologists
climbed, step by frozen step.

If they'd discovered the remains
of Noah's ark
and managed to bring scripture
out of the dark,
would explorers stop
scaling these peaks?

No Crosses, Please

They lay down crosses with flowers
next to the bloody
                    pulpit
At the Sheraton Hotel
                    in Wisconsin.

A few days ago
People were praying
                    waiting as always
for the return of their savior.

When Terry Ratzmann's
              bullets
sliced through their
              worship
Destroying the bodies of
              hopeful souls

And now again,
              as always
        everyone is asking

Why. . . . . .

POT POURRI

Van Gogh Paints in a Field of Yellow Poppies

In the twilight's gloaming, he sets up his easel
at the roadside. Blazing candles fastened
to his hatband. His paintbrush swirls a whorl
of clouds, white and blue. Luminescent streaking
stars, a crescent yellow moon sharpens against
an ever-expanding sky.

A salmon writhes against the currents,
leaping over rocks and waterfalls
guided by the earth's magnetic pull.
As the nourishment of salmon
courses through my bloodstream
the flow through my veins is interlaced
with my vision that is spellbound
by Vincent's starry night.

My eyes swim over
the thickness of the paint
as it jumps off the canvas
like a salmon leaping.
I am mesmerized by his madness.

The cycle of the salmon swimming
and the passion of the artist's brushstrokes
are the weight of history
and of living.

Mystical Epiphanies

Moon Jellyfish on Long Island Sound:
lacy silk shards of white.
A solitary mushroom bride
floats like a pink umbrella,
and undulates through the milky waters
like a ballerina ebbing in mist.

The cilia of the sea anemone
open and close: an accordion
that engulfs its inauspicious victim,
buried in oblivion.

As I peer through the glass
a pool of mirrored
floating freedom,
my aqueous reflection
moves in the water.
A pink lotus flower blooms
My thoughts are expansive.

Continuity

Something keeps bothering me.
It's the something that clicks
at the edge of my senses; a noise
a quiver, a shaken foot

that something then merges
into expectations.
My intention is broken, my
meaning to function.

And only when something
becomes nothing and my senses
remain uncalled for—
can my something emerge
unbroken.

Cassandra's Cosmos

Laugh, you will laugh
at the rivers of words
that flow
from my mouth:
the snakes of Medusa.

       Methuselah couldn't know
       the heartbeat of humanity
       tick tocking until
           the earth
      disappeared
  into the sun.

This cosmic consciousness?
Only nebulae that explode
    into black.

When you hear my words,
you'll hide like Adam
in the Garden;
or fly like Icarus,
too near the sun.

A Ghazal of Brilliantine Colors

The Seychelles Islands are jewels,
Fishes swirl—a palette of colors.

Runway models parade in haute couture
Walk—retreating in a swirl of colors.

Vincent Van Gogh painted his madness in
Passionate swirls of violent colors.

The clothes I wear are skirts, blouses and shorts
Fabrics of bright and brilliant colors.

Yes Gillian, you choose to live your life
American—in red and white and blue.

Chiaroscuro

I hold your heartbreak in my hands.
I am a mother, a daughter, a teacher a wife.

I hold your heartbreak in my hands,
a glass orb
wrapped around the weight
of your terror.

I carry your weight into the nightland
as the darkness thickens:
You don't have to face alone
that half-witted hell.
I gather you into my silence.

Disquiet

I am trapped inside
    this body
in this time and in this place

I can't go back or forward,
and your death I can't erase.

Christianity
               never answered me:
             Religions cease to please.

I cannot find the answers when I fall upon my knees.

Time
                 keeps moving forward
no matter how far back I look

Destiny is defined
by the density of darkness.

Elysian Fields

I want to be a buttercup
petals clustered
in a field of golden corolla,
tossing my head in a mass
of togetherness.

    I want to be one of the green leaves
    waving in the breeze
    laughing in the trees,
    a fertilized flower
    among the summer bees.

Not for me, the white-hooded
ladies of the Handmaid's Tale,
their shielded eyes
like blinders on a horse
staring straight ahead.

    I want to be the rain
    wet until eternity,
    dripping in company.

And in the center of Elysian Fields,
we can face the sun.

Philanderer

He nourishes himself on her woman hunger:
the poet, the sage, the businessman.
Her golden locks, papaya breasts,
she drowns in the comfort of her own nest.

Dark of night sinks into her bed,
salty tears her midnight wine.
Loud ticking of her clock just brings

                            more time.

She's waiting like a little bird,
for one more crumb,

                            one more word.

A Lady Waiting

After Vermeer's "Lady Writing"

How can I convince this man to stay?
I've been writing and re-writing this letter
all day. If begging and pleading on paper
will do it, my penmanship's pretty,
my cursive is fluid.

I sit for hours and hours in sweet
contemplation. My writing's
painstaking and slow and so neat.
I paint letters in water colors:
gold leaf for decoration.
Seal the edges in wax:
no perforation.

I'll show him I'm young, willing and flouncy.
Papers in my hair make it look bouncy.
My coat makes me look heavy,
I'll have to remove it.
Underneath, silky white, will surely
improve it.

The fact that I'm writing indeed is a sin:
He already knows how much I love him.

I'm writing this letter, what more can I say?
My servant will deliver it, then here I will stay.
I'll sit here and wait for the rest of the day.

I'll please him, he'll know it; I know how to show it.

Wedding Dishes

Mother met Mother-In-Law at Bloomingdales to choose a pattern: a gift from Mother-In-Law to Bride and Groom. Mother observed the patterns and assured Mother-in-Law that Bride didn't like florals, zigzags, or variegated colors. No. It had to be plain and simple, not *gepatzed,* or showy. That was what Bride wanted. Mother knew.

The dishes were beige fine china with a plain gold circle around the rim. The set of dishes, cups, saucers, soup bowls, and side plates served twelve.
"These dishes are for entertaining in your new home. A proper wedding gift," Mother assured Bride.

Bride and Groom lived happily in an apartment, so, Mother-In-Law agreed to keep the dishes in her basement until Bride was ready. Bride and Groom had two daughters and moved to a house in the suburbs.

Bride used the dining room to teach English lessons, and Groom did his accounting work on the table late at night. The dining room table was covered by a plastic floral table cloth; SAT books for their college-bound daughter were strewn across it.

The Floods came and Mother-In-Law insisted that Bride take her dishes. So Bride and Groom who had been happily married for twenty years schlepped the dishes into their basement, where they remained unopened, in a crate marked "Fine China" on top of an old bureau.

The Thinker

(performed as a song accompanied by guitar)

Standing alone I watch you all passing
Some go in sorrow, some take it easy
Many are heavy, yet often you all are sublime
I am the thinker, and you are the men
Who pass through the shadows of time.

Detached through the ages
Yet still from among you
I've watched people grind on the treadmill
      of life—

Still others have seen those before you and after—
The prophets and sages, yes these men are rife.

Standing alone I watch your laughter
I am the thinker and you are the men
Who pass through the shadows of time.

Natural Religion

If I were called in to construct a religion, I should make use of nature.
Going to church would entail a gathering in gardens to have each
person hold a brightly colored flower, examine the perfection of
petunias. How God in all his glory gifted us with perfectly petaled
glorious gardenias;
the quintessential quietness, the light breath of breeze caressing our
countenances, the soft summer sun encircling our shoulders.

Peace and understanding would not be woven into our psyches with
words of wisdom, but imparted with the purity of the perfection of
creation. We would not need to be pardoned from sins towards
mankind.
We would expand our vision with the vitality of naturalness and the
beauteousness of the bounty of nature. Nature stands there in all her
glory, quietly, comfortably, beautifully.

I would bow to the bougainvillea. And we, as mankind, with all our
choices would choose to hold hands together and sing *kumbaya*. We
would sing and dance, the garlands of nature encircling our necks.

Know, somehow, that if we could imitate the immaculate imagery of
God's imagination, there would be no need for wars, and creeds
or carnal deeds. We would just look into each other's eyes, and BE.

MOTHERHOOD

Unborn

Oh frozen uterus, submerged deep inside her belly
lying there, suspended in timelessness
softly sleeping, oblivious to woman's pain.
The clock ticks daily,
it soon will be too late.

Doctors interrupt the cycle
as it ebbs and flows.
Testing, probing, analyzing.
She charts her temperature daily,
waiting for a miracle.

Time, patience
medical bills mounting.
She watches children play
down by the lake.
Wanders aimlessly
past the stream,
through the gate.
It opens, she walks through,
she looks for her children
in the morning dew.

My Little Heartbeat

My little heartbeat, small round pulsing blob on the monitor; I saw you twice, ever, when the nurse squeezed out a large tube of yucky slimy gel that was oh so cold on my stomach. She slid the contraption near my belly button, and there you were: a gray moving mass. That was Tuesday. The slow brown leak kept coming into the sanitary pad. Twenty four more hours and I lay back on the hard cold table. There you were again. That was Wednesday. On Thursday, I was back in the doctor's office but this time I brought your father. He removed his Clark Kent light brown coat and hung it in the waiting room.

"I'll call you in to see the heartbeat," I said to him as I closed the door that led to the waiting room, removed my clothes for the third time that week and lay down on the hard cold table that was as familiar to me now as my own bed. The cold slimy gel was placed on my stomach; the nurse moved the contraption to the left, then, to the right. She moved the contraption up, and then she maneuvered it downwards. She never said a word. She turned off the monitor.

"I'll call the doctor," she said as she exited the room and I lay there wondering, had you joined your brother or your sister who had bled out of me just seven months before? I was thirty-six years old and childless up until this point. After the doctor came in, looked at the monitor and wrote your fate on his doctor's clipboard, I exited the examining room to see your father's hopeful face and told him, "There's nothing to see. I have to go to the hospital now."

After the DNC which cleared out my still barren womb, they placed me in the maternity ward for overnight rest. All night long I heard newborn babies crying. "Why did they put me in this ward?" I asked the nurse. "It's where he has his patients," she replied. In the morning, an orderly came in with my breakfast tray. "What did you have, a boy or a girl?" he smiled cheerily at me. "I had a miscarriage," I answered and he flew out of my room as if there were a fire in it. That afternoon my husband wheeled my chair towards the elevator for the ride home. We had to wait up for another lady in a wheelchair ahead of us. It was overburdened with presents, an infant in her arms and a balloon flying high up above her chair, pink and gray and shining with the words emblazoned on its already deflating exterior: IT'S A GIRL.

Emerge

Push, strain, bleed
pulsate. Giving life.
Reach, grow, emerge
become.
Giving woman new life
of her own.
Long, long awaited.

Her decisions fall
like droplets of water
on a parched
desert. He waits.
He is not a childless father.
Saddened by the loss
of what
might have been.

Less time, less money, no one to
help her.
Choose between being frazzled,
isolated.
A flower,
in the prime of life.
Dreaming of peace, finally.

Will a swollen belly
burst the flower?
Her ambition, a puff of smoke,
wafting into nothingness?
Or provide
a sibling?

My Rose Cherry Bundle

Cesarean cut stings
prickling as I walk
lower back aches.
Pain travels
like race cars
through my abdomen.

A bulging blocked bowel
enlarged stomach
engorged with gas.
Blood oozes slowly
from purple bruises
around the swollen veins
on my left hand
where the I.V. plummets.
Bruises dot my hips
where needles visit.

Parched lips suck
ice chips.
I crave
hospital food.

Rosy cherub cheeks
sucking in loud gulps
at my breast.
Slurping, mewling
kitten.

Head like a coconut
nestles in the crook
of my arm. Body curved,
a watermelon
across my belly.

You soak me in
with oblong grey blue
saucer eyes.
Matchstick fingers
vicelike,
gripping mine.
Curved paintbrush
eyelashes close,
my Ashley Dawn.

Summer Study Abroad

The jumbo jet rolls down the runway,
you're aerodynamically transported away from me.
The ghost of your umbilical cord aches
inside. You take one more step
towards your sovereignty. I'll think
back to the time you were three,
when everything you did depended on me.

I'll dream of you floating in the Isle
of Capri. You swim like a nymph
in the waters of Compania.
You're rowed romantically on a gondola
in the city of Venezia. A proud mama bird
I let my fledgling fly free.
Exit the parking lot at LaGuardia
and pray for your safe journey on Alitalia.

Birthright Trip

My daughter stands
on the Golan Heights,
the Israeli side
of the mountain.
Tourists sip espresso
at the nearby café
with a large *Welcome* sign.

She photographs the grassy greenery
adjacent to Syria,
and the cracked brown ground of the accursed country,
hears gunshots
every few seconds.

Her guide informs the group
of college kids
from many lands,
that each loud sound
is a mother, a father,
someone's child being ripped apart
by bullets.

A Half-Empty Nest

My body works well
except for arthritic pains scattered
throughout my hands and knees.
Especially the one that's swollen
beneath my left hand thumb.

My oldest daughter's almost a junior
in college. She dances, gets good grades.
She's happy except
her high school friend's in a coma
from O.D'ing on meth and oxytocin
and ecstasy on spring break.
Her other friend died on spring
break, also from drugs.

Then there'r the college friends
who drove drunk. Hit a tree
also dead. His passenger in a
coma. She was at a party
with them just last week.

As I walk through my house,
a half empty nest—
my other daughter
in ninth grade doesn't yet
have friends in car accidents
or overdosing on drugs.

They're still too young,
with nothing wrong
in their lives.
Give them time.

Children of Ashes

Rosy cheeked children
dancing
Soft pink rose petals
fluttering.

Til death trains
rattled them
to open graves.

Rosy cheeked children
growing healthy
unchained.
School yards filled
with chattering voices.

Nazi boots marching
herding little arms and legs
into open graves.

The smell
of flesh burning
in ovens.
Ashes to ashes.

Emaciated mothers clutching
ashes of roses.
Machine guns blasting
Silencing their forevers.

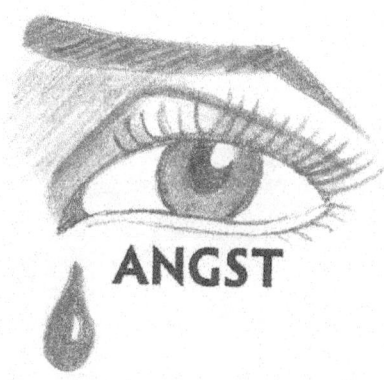

ANGST

Midnight

As a teenager, when the nightshades
were drawn and I needed
to speak to my mother,
I peeped
through her bedroom door.
It squeaked open.

My mother, propped up in bed
on plush pillows
held her finger to her mouth
with one hand, and waved me away
with the other.

I raised my hand,
a white peace flag, but my mother
motioned for me to crouch.

Johnny Carson's silent image
flickered on the television,
attached to her ear
by a long white cord.
I raised my face:
I needed questions answered.

A growl, a groan, a cough
from the other side of the bed,
a figure turning under the bedclothes—
a voice from the silence:
Who's there?

Portrait

The Galleria Mall photographer in White Plains
photographed me for the article I wrote,
"Witness to the Birth and Death of My Country."

It appeared in all the Westchester Sunday
newspapers the day I graduated
with my second Bachelor's degree
I was forty-one.
My four-year-old daughter attended
in a little white dress with a pleated skirt
and matching navy blue polka dot jacket.

I gave my mother a copy of the color portrait
eleven by fourteen, which she set
on her mahogany upright piano.

This was the same portrait that appeared
on the cover of my first book. My dress
the same color as the cover,
the burnt orange sunset
of the South African skies.

After another of our telephone arguments
she removed the portrait. Mother,
you said you didn't want me looking at you.

But I will always look at my daughter.
Her large blue eyes and soft brown curls.
I will watch as she dances
into her future, free of the invisibility
that was forced upon me.

And I always wonder. . . .
did she rend my portrait into pieces?
Or crumple it? My burnt orange dress
all scratched and wrinkled?

Did the portrait
now resemble the same squashed
face that she thrust out
between her legs on the day
that I first came into the world?

Doctor Jennifer

She walks through wards,
healing patients
when she can.
Some live
their last hours
with her.

Jack's lover brought her
a silver necklace:
thanks
for a few more
days of life.

Thirty-six hours
straight
she works.
Goes home
at shift's end,
alone.

The Practice

I was a child
and he was on the phone.
He couldn't play or
listen.

He was running
in the middle of the night
to his patients.

He said:
You have no problems.
Get in my car—
I'll drive you to see
real misery.

I was a teenager
and his beeper pierced
our conversation
in the middle of dinner.

Mother scolded:
he has no time,
he deals with death
every day.

Nothing matters
both my parents said
if it doesn't involve
The Practice.

I once had a sister
who had time
to listen.
Now she's with our father
running at night
with her beeper
to patients dying.

Hands

A twelve year old
girl
washes her
hands
until the skin
is raw

Her father
sets down
his
stethoscope
and uses
his fists
as
a cure

Her screams
echo
though
the
walls

Mother wrings
her
hands
begging:
Quiet down!
The neighbors.

In
another
room
sister irons
her
party dress.

King Lear

You broken old vessel.
Days of slumber.
Frailties never cast asunder.

Your memory unfading
of ministrations
you heaped upon the failing.

Your bloodless bones hardly hold
as you cling to her, your life raft
your wife. While your healing
hands hurt.

Half blind,
is it lamentable
to recall
your daughter—
how you beat the youth
right out of her?

And now your words bemoan
a paralyzing fate you would not
call your own.

And you carry it all
like a funeral pall.

Both Sides Now

Sitting in my aunt's garden in Johannesburg,
strumming my guitar by the pool,
singing Judy Collins' *Both Sides Now*—
She *"didn't really know life at all."*
And what did I know either, at seventeen.
Still I wrote songs and poems,
while my parents only laughed.

Mother had designed and built
the two story Colonial in Scarsdale New York
for our big move. But missing home,
we only lived there two years.

She needed my older sister to scrub floors,
to talk to in the middle of the night.
Cinderella was away at school
in upstate New York, doing well on her own:
But Mother needed her home, and got it.

At Scarsdale High, we'd read literature and poetry.
Students wrote philosophical memories in the yearbook.
But in Johannesburg, there was no time for words and song,
I studied Geography, Commerce and Afrikaans.

I lived in between.
A plane carried me from southernmost Africa
to the northeast USA.
And four years after getting settled in
I was back in my aunt's Johannesburg garden,
strumming and singing *Both Sides Now,*
still not knowing life at all.

Now, I'm in New York, again,
in between children and dishes and laundry.
I look at my life from both sides now,
mine nuggets of truth
from the zig and the zag of my youth.

Airport Nostalgia

When I embark on airport travel
memories of my youth unravel.
The journey brings me to nostalgia
and gives my nerves that old neuralgia.

The airport stores and check-in gates
greet me like some long-lost mates.
This was forever to be my fate
because of the political state.

Every time I had to travel
my life and senses would unravel.
My classmates went to junior proms
while my life shattered from the bombs.

Back and forth across the equator
my life had no administrator.
An émigré and then an émigree
depended on which side of the Atlantic sea.

We began by fleeing from apartheid
but it was my parents I began to hate.
It wasn't South African racial strife
that brought me to the changes in my life.

It was my mother's indecision,
my father gave her no derision.
So back and forth to old New York
I turned into a mixed up dork.

But many miles and cities later
I finally learned how not to hate her.
Now every time I have to fly
I harken back to times gone by.

Author photograph
Courtesy of Ray Shemer

About the Author

Gillian Lynn Katz was born in South Africa and immigrated to the United States as a teenager in 1966. She grew up in the apartheid era and has written and published extensively on that subject. In 2012 she won Second Place for her poem *Midnight* in the Greenburgh Poetry Contest. Her chapbook *Kaleidoscope* was published by Finishing Line Press that same year. She holds a Master of Arts in Writing from Manhattanville College and a Bachelor of Arts in Literature from Purchase College. She has taught creative writing and poetry to teenagers at the Scarsdale JCC in the Summer Arts Writing Program. Ms. Katz is currently working on a novel about her experience of culture shock as a teenage immigrant and the effect it had on her family.

PORTRAIT

www.ingramcontent.com/pod-product-compliance
Lightning Source LLC
Chambersburg PA
CBHW022159080426
42734CB00006B/505